How t
Grow a Part-Time
Notary Public & Loan
Signing Agent
Business

DIY STARTUP GUIDE FOR ALL 50 STATES & DC

BY

RICHARD BAILEY

Cover design

Mary Perez

First Edition

CONTENTS

PART – 1

BECOMING A NOTARY PUBLIC AND LOAN SIGNING AGENT

INTRODUCTION - THE BASICS

Notarization is something that a lot of us hear about, but aren't exactly clear on what it is and who does it. It is a little-known job that can be easily utilized to start and offer you an excellent source of side income. In this book, we are going to look at how you can get started as a Public and Loan Signing Agent and how to turn it into a successful side business to help supplement your income.

WHAT IS NOTARIZATION?

Notarization is a way to deter fraud and allow all parties in a transaction to know that a document is authentic and trustworthy. A Notary Public performs the three-part process that vets, certifies and records. Sometimes you'll hear notarizations referred to as "notarial acts."

Simply put, a notarization is an assurance from an impartial and duly appointed Notary Public that a document is authentic, the signature is genuine, and that the signer wasn't under duress or intimidation.

It helps to ensure the intended terms of a document are put into full effect and force.

The core value of notarization is the impartial screening of the Notary for a signer's identity, willingness, and awareness. This screening helps to prevent fraud and protects an individual's rights and property from forgers, identity thieves, and exploiters. Let's consider different acts that can be notarized.

NOTARIAL ACTS

An acknowledgment is an act done on documents that control or convey ownership of a valuable asset. Examples of these documents are property deeds, powers of attorney, and trusts. To complete an acknowledgment, the signer needs to be present in person and positively identified to declare that the signature is their own and that they made it willingly so that the provisions in the document can occur exactly as written.

A Jurat is often used on evidentiary documents that are important or vital to the operation of the civil and criminal justice system. This would include documents such as affidavits, depositions, and interrogatories. For these, the signer needs to appear in person to sign the document and verbally speak an oath or affirmation to promise that the statements in the document are true.

Lastly, copy certification is done to confirm that a reproduction of an original document is true, exact, and complete. This would include original documents such as college degrees, passports, and other important personal papers that only have one original and can't be copy-certified by a public record office. This form of notarization isn't authorized in every state, and in some states can only be done with certain types of original documents.

Now that we know what notarization is and the types of notarization that occur, let's briefly look at the process itself. Soon after we can start looking at who does this so you can make sure doing this job matches your needs.

The first part of a notarization process is for the Notary to screen the signer. They need to ensure the identity, but also check volition and awareness of the signer.

The second part involves the Notary entering key details in the journal of notarial acts. This chronological journal is a best practice, widely endorsed by those in the business. Record keeping itself isn't a legal requirement, but some states do require the signers to leave a signature and thumbprint in the journal.

The last part is to complete a "notarial certificate" that states the facts being certified in the notarization are in accordance with the facts. The notarization is completed with the Notary's signature and seal of office on the certificate, which is the recognized symbol of the Notary office. This symbol gives a document weight in legal matters and make it genuine in a court of law.

Now that we know about the process of notarization, we need to look at the individuals who perform the act, and the difference between a Notary Public and a Notary Signing Agent.

WHAT IS A NOTARY PUBLIC?

A Notary Public is someone appointed by the state government who is an official of integrity that serves the public as an impartial witness for a range of official fraud-deterrent acts when it comes to signing important documents. These official acts are called notarizations, or notarial acts. Notaries are commissioned publicly as "ministerial" officials, meaning they follow written rules without personal bias.

WHAT DOES A NOTARY DO?

The duty of a Notary is to screen the signers of important documents to determine their true identity, their willingness to sign without intimidation or duress, and their awareness of the contents of a transaction and/or document. Sometimes, the

Notary may need to put the signer under an oath, declaring that the information in a document is true and correct. A Notary is commonly needed for property deeds, wills, and powers of attorney.

The foundation of a Notary's trust is their impartiality. They are duty-bound to not act in a situation if they have a personal interest; Notaries do not corrupt the screening process with self-interest, but rather remain impartial and never refuse to serve someone based on race, nationality, religion, politics or sexual orientation.

Notaries Public are official representatives of the state that certify the proper execution of private citizen documents that often have life-changing weight. They help our civil society to function. Unlike Notaries in other countries, a US Notary Public is not an attorney, judge, or other high-ranking official.

WHAT IS A NOTARY SIGNING AGENT?

A Notary Signing Agent is different from a Notary. They are a Notary who is specially trained to handle and notarize loan documents. Notary Signing Agents are the link lenders use to complete a loan. They are typically hired as independent contractors in order to ensure real estate loan documents are executed by the borrower, notarized, and returned on time to be processed. This is what helps the loan to be funded.

DIFFERENCE BETWEEN A NOTARY PUBLIC AND SIGNING AGENT

Often, people use the terms Notary Public and Notary Signing Agent interchangeably, but they are actually two different positions. There are specific transactions and situations where one of these might be used over the others. Therefore, it is important to know the difference between the two to know which is the better option for you to start a side business. Let's look at how these two differ.

LEVEL OF CERTIFICATION

A Notary Public has the role of verifying the identity of an individual signing a document that needs to be executed as such under the law. These Notaries aren't required to review the content of the paperwork or determine its legality; they are simply required to apply a notary seal for the purpose of verification.

On the other hand, a Notary Signing Agent has more involvement in the actual execution of the documents when it comes to real estate. These Notaries go over the entire loan package with the borrowers, making sure all signatures are in the right place and that it is notarized as required under the law. A Notary Public who has a state-issued commission can choose to become a Notary Signing Agent by getting additional certification, which varies in requirements by state.

LEVEL OF TRAINING

A Notary Signing Agent needs to provide a greater explanation to borrowers about the documents they are signing, while a Notary Public only needs to provide verification of identity for those executing the paperwork.

This means a Notary Signing Agent needs more training and education in order to properly assist borrowers.

Specifically, a Notary Signing Agent needs to know how the entire mortgage process works, as well as specifics for their state. Some particular training includes the home loan process applicable to the state where you are working with the documents.

Now that we know what we are considering becoming let's take a look at what it takes to become a notary public and a Notary Signing Agent.

BECOMING A NOTARY PUBLIC AND LOAN SIGNING AGENT

Becoming a Notary Public in your state is a simple matter of meeting the eligibility requirements and following the required steps in your state to become commissioned. The process will vary between states, but often you fill out an application, pay a fee, take a training course and exam, file your bond and oath of office, then buy your notary supplies and start your business. Before we get into the specifics, let's take a look at the reasons why you should become a Notary Public.

5 BENEFITS OF BECOMING A NOTARY PUBLIC

Current statistics show that there is one Notary for every 72 people in the United States. That means millions of people work as Notaries Public to help protect individuals from fraud and identity theft. While doing this line of work may not be for everyone, there are a lot of benefits to consider. Not only can it be an excellent source of extra income, but it can also offer other benefits as well. Here are five main reasons why you should consider becoming a Notary Public.

Additional Income

Although Notaries are appointed by the state and serve as public officials, they directly charge clients and keep all the revenue. This is why a lot of people choose to serve as "mobile Notaries" in their community. While most states have regulations on how much you can charge for an individual notarization, most clients will need additional signatures notarized, and you are allowed to charge for additional fees such as travel time, supplies, and other expenses.

Advance to a Notary Signing Agent

If you want to become a Notary for additional income, then you can also consider advancing your career to become a Notary Signing Agent or NSA. These trained and certified professionals handle the notarization of real estate documents at closing. You are either hired directly by a title company, or you can work as an independent contractor. You can make a considerable amount of extra income if you choose to advance in this area.

Improve Skills and Resume

A number of industries view notaries as a high demand skill including banking, finance, medical, legal, government, insurance, technology, and others. The list is virtually endless. Nearly all industries use Notaries at some level, so having this skill can improve your resume and make you more valuable and marketable as an employee. Notaries serve two main functions in the workplace:

1. Notarizing back office documents for co-workers and bosses.
2. Notarizing for customers in a business setting such as a bank or a shipping shop.

Most employers will value an employee who has Notary skills. So this can even be a great way to improve your chances of finding a job.

Flexible Work Schedule

If you choose to become a mobile Notary/Notary Signing Agent, then you will be able to enjoy the flexibility of setting your own hours. This makes it an excellent option for the home-based entrepreneur, stay-at-home parents, or those looking to make little extra money from a second job. Most people who need notarizations don't mind having the service done after business hours, so you can even do your work in the evening at a time that is most convenient for you.

Assist the Community

Members of America's Notaries Public are known for helping those in need in the community. If you enjoy giving back to others in your community, then being a Notary is a great option. There are many people who need notarization services but aren't able to afford them, such as the elderly, homeless, disabled, and college students. You can choose to hold an event of your own or help out with a planned event in your community. Not only does this allow you to help your community, but it can also be a great way to market your services to paying customers.

Now that we know the reasons why you should become a Notary Public, you may be thinking this is a good option for you. If so, let's continue and see what it costs to get started as a Notary Public and Signing Agent so you can see what you need to have prepared.

THE COST OF BECOMING A NOTARY PUBLIC AND SIGNING AGENT

When it comes to start-up costs, starting a Notary business for yourself is one of the least expensive options. While it does require some financial investment, it often doesn't go beyond that of the cost of commission and certification. If you want to supplement your income by doing Notary work, then it is important that you evaluate the cost of starting your business and what you can expect to get in return.

Oftentimes, the first step in becoming a Notary and/or Signing Agent is to get the necessary training, certification, and a yearly background check in order to meet the requirements of companies who may want to hire you.

Not including your necessary supplies and commissioning costs, becoming a Notary and Signing Agent will typically cost between $140 and $200, depending on who you go to. Most packages include background screening, certification, and a training course.

In some states, there will be additional licensing requirements and/or restriction for Notaries or Signing Agents. For example, in Indiana and Maryland all closings require title insurance, and in Minnesota, you need to have a closing agent license. While certification is not required under law, it does show that the Notary has the proper training and skills to do loan document signings.

In addition, regular training will help to keep you up to date on changes with loan packages and federal regulations.

OFFICE SUPPLIES YOU WILL NEED

In addition to your Notary commission, seal, and journal, there are a few other supplies you'll want to consider getting:

- ☐ E&O Insurance
- ☐ Cell phone
- ☐ Computer or Laptop
- ☐ Dual Tray Printer
- ☐ Letter and Legal-sized paper and printer toner
- ☐ Marketing materials such as a website and business cards

Once you get started, it can be a good idea to get your Signing Agent profile listed on several company directories like Snapdocs and Signing Agent.com. Some sites will require you to pay a fee in order to be listed, and others are free. When you add your information to these directories, it allows a range of companies to find you and bring business to you such as title companies, real estate agents, and escrow companies. Make sure you keep your profile listing up to date so you can be sure you are eligible for assignments.

It is important that you make sure you have a good quality computer or laptop. These can easily cost between a few hundred dollars and $1,000 or more. You also want to have a reliable, dual-tray printer, since you are regularly going to be printing out loan packages of 100+ pages as a Loan Signing Agent. It is also a good idea to keep a well-supplied stock of both letter-sized and legal-sized paper.

Lastly, you want to make sure you have a good unlimited cell phone plan. You should find one with unlimited data, talk, and text, so you have more freedom when using your cell phone. Expect these to cost you about $50 to $100 a month.

ADDITIONAL EXPENSES TO CONSIDER

Perhaps the most difficult additional expense to quantify as a Notary is your vehicle. Since your job is going to require you to travel to multiple locations, you need to be sure you have an adequate budget set aside for keeping your vehicle in good running order. You can easily find yourself putting hundreds of miles on your car in a week, which can be quite costly in terms of gas, oil, tires, and other routine maintenance.

With everything included, it can easily cost between $1,000 to $2,000 to get started with a Notary business. It is also important to consider what you can't put a price tag on, such as the time and energy you'll have to invest in order to get your business started and to flourish to its full potential.

LEGAL RISKS TO CONSIDER

Loan document signings are very important transactions that often involve hundreds of thousands of dollars, and potentially millions. This is why it is important for a Notary to follow state laws as well as federal mortgage regulations when it comes to protecting the privacy of the signer's information.

A Loan Signing Agent needs to carefully follow proper procedure. Failing to do this could not only reduce your chances of finding work in the future, but it can also result in criminal penalties or financial liability.

REQUIRED CERTIFICATION AND TRAINING

To become a Signing Agent, there is no certification required by law. However, many companies will ask for Signing Agents they work with to be certified and background-checked according to Consumer Financial Protection Bureau compliance requirements for a third-party service provider that is hired through financial institutions. You can get certification, training, and background screening through several private organizations.

The following states do require training for Notaries:

- ☐ California
- ☐ Colorado
- ☐ Florida
- ☐ Missouri

☐ Montana

☐ Nevada

☐ North Carolina

☐ Oregon

☐ Pennsylvania

In addition, the state of Delaware requires both training and continuing education in order to do electronic Notaries.

Any state that requires Notary training needs the applicant to be approved by the state. This means that as long as you take a state-approved course, you will be taught the basics that are entailed by the state. Even if the majority of states don't call for training or education, they do support voluntary education.

The first place to go for training is the Notary-regulating agency within your state. This is typically the Secretary of State's office. You may also find Notary education at your local community colleges.

There is also a large number of organizations and vendors that offer training online as well, such as the

National Notary Association. No matter what training you choose, it will help you to become confident in your duties as you start on a career in Notaries public.

NOTARY EXAMINATION BY STATE

In most states, you aren't required to take an exam to become a Notary. The states that do need you to pass a test are the following:

- ☐ California
- ☐ Colorado
- ☐ Connecticut
- ☐ Hawaii
- ☐ Louisiana
- ☐ Maine
- ☐ Montana
- ☐ Nebraska
- ☐ New York
- ☐ North Carolina
- ☐ Oregon
- ☐ Utah

In Wyoming, applicants are encouraged to take an in-home test, but it isn't a requirement. In Ohio, there is no statewide exam— but it may be required by local judges or committees.

If you live in a state that requires an exam, they typically take about an hour. The exam may or may not include fingerprinting to submit along with your state Notary application once you've completed the exam.

BACKGROUND CHECK

There are some states where it is a requirement to have a background check done before becoming a Notary. Some states that don't require a background check may request one if you have ever been convicted of a misdemeanor or felony. However, if you choose to become a Loan Signing Agent, it is a different story.

In order to become a Loan Signing Agent, you need to have a background check. You are given access to private financial information, and within the mortgage industry, all individuals involved in the lending process must undergo a background check.

BONDS & E&O INSURANCE

In most states, you will need a Notary bond to do business. At the time of writing this, 30 states and the District of Columbia require a Notary to have a surety bond in order to do business, but the amount of this bond varies greatly by state. The average range is between $5,000 to $10,000— but some states can be as low as $500 and as high as $25,000.

The surety bond helps to protect consumers. Should you make a mistake that damages someone, the bond will help compensate the injured person up to the amount of the bone. You would then be required to repay the company issuing the bond.

On the other hand, liability insurance isn't required since your state doesn't write Notary laws to protect Notaries, but instead to protect the public. This is why many states require bonds. Although it is a good idea to buy a Notary errors and omissions insurance policy since it protects you against any claims made relating to any errors made during a notarization.

The Signing Professionals Workgroup (SPW) that sets industry standards recommends having an E&O policy of $25,000 since most claims against Notaries average about $14,000. Although, some companies may have requirements for signing agents to carry a larger policy.

COST OF INSURANCE AND BONDS

The cost of becoming a Notary can vary greatly. In some states, it can be less than $100 while in others it can easily be several hundreds of dollars. This is because each state has a different application filing fee and the cost of training, exams, background screenings, and bonds/insurance can vary greatly depending on requirements.

EQUIPMENT

Typically, a Notary is going to need three main supplies: certificates, a seal for stamping certificates, and a journal for keeping a record of all notarizations completed. Many states no longer require a Notary to keep a journal, but you may choose to keep one for both your protection and that of the public.

Perhaps the most difficult supply is the certificates since that are different types of notarizations that each require their own type of certificate. You can often get basic certificates online through state Notary-regulating sites, but these may not give the impression you want to make at a signing. For a more professional appearance, some suppliers have certificates online so you can download the right certificate you need rather than keeping a stock of paper certificates available if the occasion calls for it.

It is important to remember that just because a piece of equipment isn't required by your state, it doesn't mean you can't use it in your business. There are a lot of Notary supplies available online that can help you do your job, protect you, and make things easier for you. So, take the time to look around and find out what you need specifically.

In addition to the three basics above that most Notaries are going to need, a Signing Agent will also necessitate reliable transportation in order to get to and from assignments, a good mobile phone, and a business email address to communicate between signers and companies. It is also helpful to have a printer and fax machine so you can print the necessary loan documents and fax any required documents.

So if you still think starting a Notary is for you, then let me give you five tips you need in order to successfully achieve your goal.

5 TIPS FOR STARTING A NOTARY BUSINESS

Once you get your Notary commission, you'll want to get started in your new business right away. However, it can be confusing as to what comes next.

So I'm going to share with you five tips to help you get your Notary business off on the right start.

BEGIN WITH WHAT YOU KNOW

The best place to start is by focusing on what you know, then building your business one service at a time. Often, those new to the Notary career will try several different services right away, such as loan signings, general consumer work, loan modifications, auto loans, etc.

However, if you are new and don't have experience in all these areas, it can be easier to make a mistake that hurts your business and costs you future work. Instead, you should start with just one or two services to get familiar and comfortable with them.

Once you have gained sufficient experience to do the job well, you can add more services in order to increase your business. Just make sure you don't overextend yourself since that causes mistakes which in turn leads to loss of work and revenue.

CONNECT WITH OTHERS

It can be very important to find a Notary who would like to mentor you. It should ideally be someone within your state that can provide guidance, support, and the ideas you need in order to build a thriving business. Working with a mentor can also be a great way to get jobs; you will be able to help with their overflow assignments, and you can refer projects to them if they are outside of your comfort zone.

In addition to a mentor, you should also try to network with other Notary professionals in your state. This can help you increase your business without having to pay excess marketing costs. People prefer to do business with those they trust, and networking is all about building relationships. Many of the Notaries that have long-term success are those who use Notary networks.

CONTINUING EDUCATION

The rules and laws that govern Notaries are constantly changing, the same as expectations for Signing Agents. In order to avoid mistakes and to keep your business thriving, you need to keep up to date on these changes through continuing education. There are three things you can do for your continuing education that are going to have a dramatic impact on your business.

First, read and review the guide for Notaries in your state. In most states, you are able to download and print all the current laws for Notaries.

Second, look for both local as well as national workshops and conferences that give you presentations and training to help you improve your knowledge in the Notary profession.

Third, check with professional Notary associations or your state commissioning office to get answers to any Notary-related questions.

STICK TO YOUR BUSINESS PLAN

Whether you are just starting out as a Notary or if you've been doing the job for a while, you need to have a plan if you want to be successful. A business plan is the best way to anticipate and overcome both financial and legal obstacles that can occur over time, even those that may not seem obvious at first.

Developing the right business plan can help you both start and expand your business while also knowing what resources will help with your success. A business plan also allows you to charge appropriately for your services, and create the right type of business model you should develop.

MARKET APPROPRIATELY

Having a strong marketing plan is the key to a successful business. Marketing for Notaries has changed a lot in recent years. Notaries used to be able to make a decent income from a simple profile posted online and then getting calls from potential customers, but this isn't the case anymore.

Instead, you need to develop a strategy in order to spread the word about your Notary services. It is important to do this both online as well as within your local community. In addition to family and friends, be sure to spread the word that you offer Notary services to professionals in local businesses, schools, churches, insurance agencies, banks, and real estate offices.

However, you also want to make sure you advertise your Notary business online through social media platforms such as Facebook, LinkedIn, and Twitter. If you intend to become a Loan Signing Agent, then you also want to make sure you have a profile on sites such as SigningAgent.com and keep your information up to date.

Once you've got everything in place to get your Notary business started, you can start taking jobs. This is when you need to give consideration to how you will run your new business working as a Notary. Let's take a look at some helpful tips, starting with how you will be able to get your first assignment.

RUNNING A NOTARY PUBLIC AND LOAN SIGNING AGENT BUSINESS

GETTING YOUR FIRST ASSIGNMENT

The first thing you'll likely ask yourself once you've got everything set up and ready to go is, how do you get your first assignment? There isn't a simple and direct answer to this question.

Even after you've researched the market, developed an excellent business plan, and started networking with other Notaries in your area; there is still a lot more you need to do in order to get your first assignment. Here are some tips that can help you.

KNOW THE MARKET

The first thing you need to do is determine what type of businesses you want to attract as clients. With just a little research you'll realize that not all title and signing companies hire Notaries and do business in the same way. It is important that you do a lot of comparisons and ask a lot of questions.

Doing this will give you a good idea of the companies that are the best fit for you to do business with. Once you know your potential clients, the next part of the process becomes a little easier. It is best to have two different plans in place: one for businesses within your state, and one for businesses out-of-state.

It is important to have these two different plans since title/signing companies use different methods when it comes to finding qualified Notaries for their specific needs. Let's look at out-of-state clients first.

GETTING OUT-OF-STATE CLIENTS

There are three steps to take that can help you get Notary assignments from out-of-state clients.

First, go to websites that allow you to create a professional Notary profile such as SigningAgent.com. Through these sites, you are able to create a profile that potential customers can view. You should check out some of the other more experienced profiles first to see what you should include in your own. It is important that you always place emphasis on your strengths.

The second step is to meet up with other professional Notaries within your state. Networking with other professionals in your business field will allow you to take on assignments from other overwhelmed Notaries and it will give you help when you need someone to assist. Having a mentor within the field is also going to make it easier for you to get your Notary business started, as was previously mentioned.

Lastly, you want to attend national conferences for Notaries. The vendors at these events are typically national title/signing companies who are looking for Notaries open to new clients. The best option for someone new to the business is the annual conference held by the National Notary Association. This gives you a chance to build a reputation with national companies that can give you a lot of out-of-state business.

IN-STATE CLIENTS

When it comes to getting in-state clients, there are a few things you can do as well.

If you want to get loan assignments, you should go to your bank or other financial institution and ask to be referred to the title company they use for loan assignments. This can be the quickest way to get a referral for loan signing assignments.

Another option is to go to title companies in your area and do a survey. This can be an effective way to get business from title companies. Go to you title company with a clipboard and ask a few survey questions such as the following:

- Do you use Notary Signing Agents?
- What makes you hire a Notary Signing Agent?
- What is your biggest issue when using a Notary Signing Agent?

This can give you a good idea of the companies you want to do business with. It can also help you see what they are looking for to increase your chances of getting hired.

You should also attend local land title functions in your local area. Type your state and Land Title Association into a search browser, and you'll find the website for your local land title association website. From this website, you'll see all the local events in your area. Attending these events will give you a chance to expose yourself to those seeking Notaries and Loan Signing Agents.

Getting your first assignment as a Notary can seem daunting at first, but once you set a goal and focus on getting the project in case, you'll be able to get a great one. After you get a few under your belt, it will become easier to get new assignments and build them into a thriving Notary business. However, it is also important that you know and understands what companies are looking for to help improve your chances of getting hired.

WHAT COMPANIES LOOK FOR

Once you have secured your first assignment, you will want to find more work. There are several things you can do to set yourself apart from other Notaries and encourage more business. Let's look at the things companies look for when hiring Notaries so you can be prepared to get additional assignments.

BE A PROFESSIONAL

From the time you take a call to the time you return a package, you are clocked in as a working professional. Sometimes you may be the only person fact borrowers see when it comes to their mortgage. This is a big responsibility, and you don't want to take it lightly.

No matter what circumstances you find yourself in, you want to act professionally. Whether a signing takes place in an office, at home or outside in your car, you always want to give a professional appearance and sound.

Always dress as if you are going to be working in an office. Speak to others in a way that demonstrates your knowledge about the documents and show that you are helping them through the process. Never talk bad about any other companies, whether it be the signing company, bank, or Title Company. This is never acceptable under any circumstances.

Make sure you always return all calls. Even if you can't accommodate a signing, give a callback and let them know that. You interact with a number of businesses every day and word spreads, so treat everyone the same whether they are a client or not.

Lastly, it can't be said enough; you need to constantly educate yourself. Keep up with any changes in your state for Notaries. The title and mortgage industries don't stay stagnant, but rather are always changing. When you stay on top of these changes your knowledge base will help open new job assignments to you. The more professional you are, the more good word spreads about you, and the more work you can get done.

HAVE THE RIGHT EQUIPMENT

Whether you are a Notary or a Signing Agent, you always need to be prepared for all situations you may face. It isn't enough to simply have a cell phone and the three basics we already discussed. You need to have the ability to complete any job: large or small, in person or electronic. You need to be able to properly protect people's privacy. Many Notaries lack in this area, and it doesn't leave a good impression on companies looking to hire someone.

Make sure you have a range of packing materials so you can send closing documents back in the fastest way possible. Keep up to date on renewing your appropriate licenses and insurance requirements for your state. Companies are going to go with the Notary or Signing Agent that can get the job done right away, not someone they have to wait on to get things together first.

Assist Others

Lastly, it can't be said enough that you need to develop relationships with other Notaries and Signing Agents in your area. If you can't do business with someone, but know of someone who can, then you are showing a team spirit and many businesses like this.

Keep a list of companies you had a positive experience with and spread the word about them. Even if you may lose a few assignments, you will get more, in the long run, doing it this way rather than hoarding all the business for yourself. If you don't work with others, you'll quickly become the Notary no one wants to do business with.

Always remember that you are the face of your business and you represent a huge industry. Always conduct yourself in a manner that makes companies want to call you first for business;
always make companies want to come back to you again.

Doing these things, you will be able to grow your business easily. However, there are also other areas where you can branch out as a Notary and Notary Signing Agent to get additional workflow as well. Let's look at eight popular areas that Notaries can branch out to in order to add additional income.

8 WAYS TO MAKE EXTRA MONEY

Once you have the job of a Notary down and have branched off into loan signing, you may find yourself wondering what is next. Where else can you expand your business in order to get additional assignments? There are actually eight great side jobs that a Notary can do based on their skills to make some additional income. Let's look at these eight areas.

FIELD INSPECTIONS

These are the individuals who verify information about businesses. You will be sent to a location in order to verify that they are a valid business. You may also be required to look at their business license, talk to the manager, or take photos of the office.

Most field inspectors don't need any previous qualifications, but may need to go through a background check. Training is often done briefly and over the phone. Most inspections will require you to have a high speed internet connection and a digital camera with time and date stamp capability. You'll also need a reliable vehicle. If you are doing a mobile Notary or loan signings then you most likely already have two of these things.

A typical business verification inspection will often pay $18 to $40 and only takes you about 10-15 minutes, turning this into something you can easily do while driving between appointments for your Notary business.

If you are interested, visit the website for the Society of Field Inspectors to help you get started.

PROCESS SERVERS

These are the individuals who serve legal documents like subpoenas and other court-related materials. The laws for this position vary based on the state you live in, so you'll need to look up your specific state laws. There are some jurisdictions that will require a fee in order to become a process server, while in others you'll only have to pay for a background check. There may also be a bond requirement or licensing and testing costs. It is important to note that there may be some upfront cost before you add this option to your career path.

The amount of fees you get paid will vary depending on your jurisdiction. If you are interested in branching out to this option, then you can contact the National Association of Professional Process Servers for more information on the local requirements and state associations that you can join.

VIRTUAL ASSISTANT

A virtual assistant is an independent contractor that works from home or an office in order to provide clients with different services such as bookkeeping, event planning, data processing, or administrative support.

The qualifications you need will vary depending on your abilities. It is best for those with strong communications and writing skills who are also known for being self-disciplined to work and meet deadlines without supervision.

How much you are paid will depend on the services you provide and how much you charge. If you are interested in adding this to your resume, check out the website for the International Virtual Assistants Association for more information.

PERSONAL CONCIERGE

A personal concierge is similar to a virtual assistant in the fact that it is an individual who provides a range of services such as booking travel and restaurant reservations to grocery shopping and waiting in line at places like the DMV. You can set your own fees based on the services you offer and what you negotiate with clients based on what the market allows.

There is no special training required, but you can go through a certification program. You will also need a car and a flexible schedule, the same as you need to be a mobile Notary. If you are interested in branching out to this service, then you can visit the National Concierge Association website for more information and some mentor programs to get you started.

FORM I-9 SERVICES

Every employer needs to complete a Form I-9 whenever they hire an employee. Since there is a greater number of remote employees, employers are able to designate an authorized representative to complete forms for them. Notaries are viewed as good candidates for this role according to the US Citizenship and Immigration Services.

There is no set fee for this service. However, since it isn't a Notarial act, you can often negotiate fees with each individual client based on the amount of work. There is no special training for this job, but you should be familiar with the I-9 form and the tasks required as an employer's representative.

To get started you should advertise your services on your website and various social media platforms. You can also reach out to businesses that are likely to hire remote employees.

WEDDING OFFICIANT

These are individuals who conduct marriage ceremonies for a fee. You not only perform the actual wedding ceremony, but you are also responsible for completing and filing the wedding documents with the correct vital records division in the appropriate time frame after the ceremony is complete.

In Florida, Maine, Nevada, and South Carolina you are allowed to perform marriage ceremonies as a part of your official Notary duties. Nevada requires you to apply for permission up to five times per year. In most other states, Notaries are allowed to apply for a separate license to perform a wedding ceremony. The specific licensing requirements vary by state.

How much you are able to charge varies by the state. For example, in Nevada, it is $75 while South Carolina allows $5 and travel fees.

If this sounds like an additional job you want to do, then check with your state's notary regulating agency or the county clerk's office for more information.

MYSTERY SHOPPING

A mystery shopper is someone who visits a business as a customer, then provides details about their experience and feedback. Assignments can be as varied as a quick stop at a convenience store to dining at a restaurant or even staying overnight at a hotel.

Anyone can become a mystery shopper, but those that are highly sought after are people who are detail-oriented, observant, and punctual. These are all traits that most Notaries have.

Payment can range from $5 for a quick store purchase to $200 or more for overnight hotel stays. Most mystery shoppers get started by registering with a provider company that issues assignments in their area.

You can also get started by visiting the website of the Mystery Shopping Providers Association. However, you should stay away from any companies that ask you to pay them in exchange for work. You should never have to pay for mystery shopping assignments.

UBER DRIVER

Uber is a ridesharing service that pairs riders with drivers through a smartphone app. Those who need a ride place a request through the app, which then alerts available drivers in the area that they can provide transportation for a fee. You should have access to a four-door vehicle and pass a background check.

Payment for an Uber ride can vary depending on the distance you travel, the time involved, the time of day, and the type of vehicle you drive. The advantage is you don't have any set schedules to pick up passengers. You can simply turn on the app whenever you want to make yourself available for fares.

To get started, submit your name and contact information through the online application process. You can even sign up through a partner link on the

National Notary Associations website. This gets you a $50 reward after you complete your first trip.

These are just eight of the top side jobs you can do to make extra money while working as a Notary. However, there is no shortage of options for you to make extra money on the side. But let's get back to the Notary business and look at the general steps involved in becoming a Notary and Loan Signing Agent.

HOW TO BECOME A NOTARY: STEP BY STEP

Although the procedures for becoming a Notary vary by state, which is covered at the end of this book in the state by state guide, the general steps to becoming a Notary are the same:

1. Make sure you meet the qualifications for your state.
2. Complete your application and submit to the appropriate organization.
3. Pay the required state filing fee.

4. If needed, get training from an approved vendor.
5. If needed, pass a state-required exam.
6. If needed, complete a background check and fingerprinting.
7. Receive a commission certificate from the state organization overseeing the process.
8. If needed, get your surety bond.
9. File your commission paperwork and bond with the regulating Notary official in your state.
10. Buy your required and necessary supplies.

HOW TO BECOME A LOAN SIGNING AGENT: STEP BY STEP

In order to start the Notary Signing Agent certification process, you first need to be a Notary Public. There are some states where the process of loan signings are restricted or limited. We'll discuss these in a moment. While the process to become a Notary Signing Agent varies by state, the general process to become a Notary Signing Agent is the same:

1. First review the list of state requirements and restrictions to ensure it is something you can do in your state.
2. Meet the requirements of the title company and/or signing service you plan to work for. This often includes getting Notary Signing Agent certified and background screened.
3. You should take a training course that can help you understand the duties of a Signing Agent and learn the contents of a basic loan document package.
4. Purchase the necessary supplies you need for your job.
5. Consider joining a professional organization to help you stay up to date on changes in the industry.
6. Promote yourself through signing agent databases so companies can find and hire you.
7. Start your new job as a Notary Signing Agent.

STATE BY STATE RESTRICTIONS FOR LOAN SIGNING AGENTS

If you live in any of the following states, carefully consider their restrictions before you decide to become a Loan Signing Agent. At the very least, you might have to learn special procedures; at the worst, you may go through training to offer a service you can't do in your state.

Connecticut - An attorney's signature is required for a title policy, but doesn't require attorneys to close real estate transactions. However, by custom, attorneys close most transactions. Notary Signing Agents are called on for document signings when it comes to residential refinances, home equity lines of credit, and reverse mortgages.

Delaware - Requires an attorney who is admitted to the state bar be present or involved in closing all real estate transactions.

Georgia - Requires an attorney who is admitted to the state bar be present or involved in closing all real estate transactions.

Indiana - Requires a title insurance license for all loan closings.

Maryland - Requires a title insurance license for all loan closings.

Massachusetts - An attorney admitted to the state bar is required to be present or involved in the closing of all real property transactions. A Notary employed by a lender may notarize a document related to a closing of his or her employer's real estate loans.

Minnesota - Requires a closing agent license.

Nebraska - Places limits on the fees a Notary can charge. Cannot charge any ancillary fees, such as a courier fee.

Nevada - Places limits on the fee a Notary can charge. This includes an hourly travel fee based upon the time of day you travel.

New York - Companies that hire signing professionals for assignments can choose to use only licensed attorneys.

North Carolina - Places limits on the fees a Notary can charge. Cannot charge ancillary fees.

South Carolina - An attorney admitted to the state bar needs to be present or involved in all real property transaction closings.

South Dakota - Various authorities do not allow non-attorneys to conduct signings.

Texas - Home Equity Line of Credit loans must be signed and closed in a lender, attorney, or title company office only.

Vermont - An attorney admitted to the state bar is required to be present or involved when closing real property transactions.

Virginia - Notaries cannot conduct a real property signing without an escrow license if they handle money related to closing costs.

West Virginia - An attorney admitted to the state bar needs to be present or involved in the closing of all real property transactions.

Lastly, you want to consider the renewal process to keep your Notary commission current.

HOW TO RENEW

While renewal procedures will differ depending on your state, the general process is the same:

1. Complete any state required testing and/or training.
2. Fill out a Notary application and submit.
3. Purchase and file your bond where required.
4. Receive your commission.
5. Order your Notary seal and any necessary supplies.
6. Start taking assignments.

Now that we know all of the basics let's take a look at the specifics of each state.

PART - 2

STATE BY STATE REQUIREMENTS

ALABAMA

Overseen By:

- Alabama Secretary of State. However, the probate judge in each county sets the rules and procedures for applications.

State Qualifications:

1. Must possess all legal requirements to be an officer in the state.
2. Must be a resident of the county you are applying for.
3. Residents of another state can't apply for Alabama commission.
4. A convicted felon cannot apply unless a pardon restores civil and political rights.
5. The county probate judge must approve the application and bond.

Cost:

- $10 filing fee and any required county costs.

Time Frame:

- Process an application takes 4-6 weeks.

Training:

- At the discretion of the county probate judge.

Exam:

- No state required exam, but can be required by individual probate judges.

Fingerprint and Background Check:
- No specific requirements.

Bond/Insurance:
- Requires a $25,000 surety bond.
- Insurance is not required by the state.

Equipment:
- Inking stamp or embosser.

Length of Commission:
- 4 years

ALASKA

Overseen By:

- Office of Lieutenant Governor

State Qualifications:

1. Must be 18 years of age.
2. Must be a legal US Resident.
3. Must reside in Alaska for at least 30 days, with intent to remain indefinitely.
4. Able to read, write, and understand English.
5. No conviction or incarceration for a felony within 10 years prior to commission.

Cost:

- The state filing fee is $40.

Time Frame:

- Within 4 weeks.

Training:

- Training is not required in the state of Alaska.

Exam:

- No written exam is required in the state of Alaska.

Fingerprint and Background Check:

- No specific requirements in the state of Alaska.

Bond/Insurance:

- A $1,000 four-year bond is required.
- No insurance requirements.

Equipment:

- An inked stamp or photocopiable embosser.

Length of Commission:

- 4 years.

ARIZONA

Overseen By:

- Secretary of State Office

State Qualifications:

1. Must be at least 18 years old.
2. Be able to read and write English.
3. Must be a citizen or legal permanent resident of the United States.
4. Be a legal resident of Arizona.
5. Cannot be a felon unless a pardon restores civil and political rights.

Cost:

- $43 filing fee.
- Optional $25 expedited fee.

Time Frame:

- 3-4 weeks
- 1-2 days for expedited

Training:

- No training is required by the state of Arizona.

Exam:

- There is no state required exam.

Fingerprint and Background Check:

- No official requirements.

Bond/Insurance:

- A $5,000 surety bond is required.
- No insurance is required.

Equipment:

- A rubber stamp ink seal.
- An embosser can work as a secondary seal, but cannot be the only seal.

Length of Commission:

- 4 years

ARKANSAS

Overseen By:

- Secretary of State.

State Qualifications:

1. Must be at least 18 years old.
2. Must be a US citizen or permanent resident alien.
3. Must be a legal resident of Arkansas, or employed in Arkansas and a resident of a neighboring state.
4. Must be able to read and write English.
5. No revoked Notary commission in the last 10 years.
6. Never been convicted of a felony.

Cost:

- $20 filing fee

Time Frame:

- Varies

Training:

- Training is not a state requirement.

Exam:

- A state exam isn't required.

Fingerprint and Background Check:

- No state requirements.

Bond/Insurance:

- A $7,500 10-year surety bond is required.
- Insurance is not required by the state.

Equipment:

- An ink stamp or embosser.

Length of Commission:

- 10 years

CALIFORNIA

Overseen By:

- Secretary of State

State Qualifications:

1. Be a legal resident of the state of California.
2. Be at least 18 years-old.
3. Complete a state-approved training course.
4. Pass a state prescribed exam.
5. Pass a background check.
6. Cannot have committed a felony, a crime of moral turpitude, or a crime linked to Notary duties.

Cost:

- $40 application fee

Time Frame:

- 2 weeks to six months

Training:

- A six-hour state-approved training course is required.

Exam:

- A written, proctored exam by a private company is required.

Fingerprint and Background Check:

- Both fingerprints and a background check are required by the state of California.

Bond/Insurance:

- A $15,000 surety bond is required.
- Insurance is not required.

Equipment:

- An ink stamp
- A well-bound journal

Length of Commission:

- 4 years

COLORADO

Overseen By:

- Secretary of State

State Qualifications:

1. Be at least 18 years-old.
2. Be a citizen, permanent legal resident, or lawfully present in the United States.
3. Be a resident or employee of the state of Colorado.
4. Be able to read and write in English.
5. No conviction of a felony or an unauthorized practice of law.
6. No conviction of a misdemeanor involving dishonesty in the last five years.
7. No acts of fraud, dishonesty, or deceit.
8. No revoked Notary Public commission in another state.

Cost:

- $10 filing fee

Time Frame:

- 3-5 days

Training:

- An approved two-hour class is required in the state of Colorado.

Exam:

- A 25-30 minute, online and open-book exam is required in the state of Colorado.

Fingerprint and Background Check:

- No state requirements.

Bond/Insurance:

- A bond and insurance are not required in the state of Colorado.

Equipment:

- Rubber stamp ink seal.
- A journal is also required.

Length of Commission:

- 4 years

CONNECTICUT

Overseen By:

- Secretary of State

State Qualifications:

1. Must be 18 years of age.
2. Reside or have a place of business in Connecticut.
3. Able to read, write, and understand English.
4. No felony conviction or revoked Notary commission.

Cost:

- $120 filing fee

Time Frame:

- Varies

Training:

- Not required in Connecticut.

Exam:

- You must pass a written exam in Connecticut.

Fingerprint and Background Check:

- No state requirements.

Bond/Insurance:

- No bond or insurance is required in Connecticut.

Equipment:

- No specific requirements.

Length of Commission:

- 5 years

DELAWARE

Overseen By:

- Secretary of State

State Qualifications:

1. Must be 18 years-old.
2. Maintain legal residence in Delaware, or be a non-resident worker in Delaware.
3. Have a "reasonable need" for a Notary commission.
4. Have a "good character and reputation."
5. A valid email address.

Cost:

- $60 filing fee

Time Frame:

- Varies

Training:

- Not required in Delaware.

Exam:

- Not required in Delaware.

Fingerprint and Background Check:

- No state requirements.

Bond/Insurance:

- No bond or insurance is required in the state of Delaware.

Equipment:
- Black-inked rubber stamp or embosser.

Length of Commission:
- 2 years then you can renew for 2 or 4-year commissions.

DISTRICT OF COLUMBIA

Overseen By:

- Office of Notary Commissions and Authentications

State Qualifications:

1. Must be 18 years-old.
2. Reside in Washington D.C. or work in the area.
3. Able to read, write, and understand English.
4. No felony convictions.
5. No revocation of Notary commission.

Cost:

- $75 filing fee

Time Frame:

- 6-8 weeks

Training:

- A mandatory orientation is required within three weeks of submitting your application.

Exam:

- Not required in the District of Columbia.

Fingerprint and Background Check:

- No requirement in the District of Columbia.

Bond/Insurance:

- A $2,000 five-year bond is required.

- No insurance requirements.

Equipment:

- Inked embosser containing a circular border with the following required writing:
  - ☐ In the upper, outer perimeter - your name as it appears on your commission.
  - ☐ In the center, "Notary Public."
  - ☐ In the center, your commission expiration date.
  - ☐ In the bottom, outer perimeter - "District of Columbia."
- Embossment inker
- Jurat stamp

Length of Commission:

- Varies

FLORIDA

Overseen By:

- Department of State

State Qualifications:

1. Must be 18 years of age.
2. A legal resident of Florida.
3. Cannot be a convicted felon unless civil rights have been restored.

Cost:

- $39 filing fee

Time Frame:

- Varies

Training:

- A three-hour state approved training course is required.

Exam:

- No state exam is required.

Fingerprint and Background Check:

- No state requirement.

Bond/Insurance:

- A $7,500 surety bond is required.
- No requirement for insurance.

Equipment:

- A rubber stamp that uses photographically reproducible black ink.

Length of Commission:

- 4 years

Overseen By:

- Clerk of Superior Court for your county

State Qualifications:

1. Must be 18 years-old.
2. Must reside in the state.
3. Must be a US citizen or legal resident of the US.
4. Must be a resident of the county you apply.
5. Provide an operating telephone number.
6. Be able to read and write English.

Cost:

- $37 filing fee

Time Frame:

- Varies based on county office.

Training:

- No required training, but the Secretary of State offers free orientation courses.

Exam:

- Not required in the state of Georgia.

Fingerprint and Background Check:

- No state requirements.

Bond/Insurance:

- Neither a bond nor insurance is required by the state of Georgia.

Equipment:

- Stamp or embosser that must include the following:
  - ☐ Your name
  - ☐ The words "Notary Public."
  - ☐ The words "Georgia" or "GA."
  - ☐ The name of the county where you are commissioned

Length of Commission:

- Varies

HAWAII

Overseen By:

- State Director of Finance

State Qualifications:

1. Must be 18 years-old.

2. Must reside in Hawaii.

3. Must be a US citizen, US national, or permanent alien resident authorized to work in the US.

4. Able to read, write, and understand English.

5. Not addicted to, dependent on, or habitual user of narcotics, barbiturates, amphetamines, hallucinogens, opium, cocaine, or other drugs or derivatives.

Cost:

- $10 filing fee
- $40 commission fee

Time Frame:

- 30 days

Training:

- State training is not required.

Exam:

- You are required to pass a state exam.

Fingerprint and Background Check:

- No state requirements.

Bond/Insurance:

- A $1,000 four-year bond is required.
- No insurance requirements.

Equipment:

- Inked stamp or embosser, but not both. Must have the following:
  - ☐ Circular shape
  - ☐ Serrated or milled edge border
  - ☐ Your name
  - ☐ Commission number
  - ☐ "Notary Public"
  - ☐ "State of Hawaii"

Length of Commission:

- Varies

Overseen By:

- Secretary of State

State Qualifications:

1. Must be 18 years-old.
2. Must be able to read and write.
3. Must reside or be employed in Idaho.
4. Must be a US citizen or a permanent legal resident.

Cost:

- $30 filing fee

Time Frame:

- Varies

Training:

- No state requirement.

Exam:

- No state requirement.

Fingerprint and Background Check:

- No state requirement.

Bond/Insurance:

- A $10,000 six-year surety bond is required.
- No insurance requirement.

Equipment:

- Inked stamp with serrated or milled edge border in a rectangle or circle shape. Must contain the following:
  - ☐ "Notary Public"
  - ☐ Your name
  - ☐ "State of Idaho"

Length of Commission:

- Varies

ILLINOIS

Overseen By:

- Secretary of State

State Qualifications:

1. Be a US citizen or lawful permanent resident.
2. An Illinois resident, or employed in the state and a resident of a neighboring state for at least 30 days.
3. Provide a date of birth.
4. Be able to read and write in English.
5. Not be convicted of a felony.
6. No previous revocation of Notary commission or suspension within the last 10 years.

Cost:

- $10 filing fee

Time Frame:

- 5-8 weeks

Training:

- No state requirement.

Exam:

- No state requirement.

Fingerprint and Background Check:

- No state requirement.

Bond/Insurance:

- A $5,000 four-year surety bond is required.
- No insurance requirements.

Equipment:

- Notary seal stamp.
- A journal is required if you charge fees for your services.

Length of Commission:

- Varies

Overseen By:

- Secretary of State

State Qualifications:

1. Must be 18 years-old.
2. Be a resident or primarily employed in Indiana.
3. Not hold a federal or state government position.
4. No criminal conviction with imprisonment over six months.

Cost:

- $5 filing fee
- $18.87 application fee

Time Frame:

- A couple of business days.

Training:

- A state-approved training course is required.

Exam:

- A state exam of 30 multiple choice and true-false questions is required.

Fingerprint and Background Check:

- No state requirements.

Bond/Insurance:

- A $25,000 surety bond is required.
- No insurance requirements.

Equipment:

- Inked stamp or embosser.

Length of Commission:

- 8 years

IOWA

Overseen By:

- Secretary of State

State Qualifications:

1. Must be 18 years-old.
2. Be a US citizen or permanent legal resident.
3. Known for good character, integrity, and abilities.
4. Live or work in the state of Iowa.
5. Be able to read and write English.
6. No conviction of a felony for fraud, dishonesty, or deceit.

Cost:

- $30 application fee

Time Frame:

- 4-6 weeks

Training:

- No state requirements.

Exam:

- No state requirements.

Fingerprint and Background Check:

- No state requirements.

Bond/Insurance:

- No surety bond or insurance requirements.

Equipment:

- Rubber stamp or embosser.
- Notary journal is required.

Length of Commission:

- 3 years for an Iowa resident.
- 1 year for a resident of a neighboring state.

KANSAS

Overseen By:

- Secretary of State

State Qualifications:

1. Must be 18 years-old.
2. US and Kansas resident, or a resident of a neighboring state employed in Kansas.
3. Able to read, write, and understand English.
4. No felony convictions.
5. No revocation of a professional license.

Cost:

- $25 filing fee

Time Frame:

- Varies

Training:

- No state requirement.

Exam:

- No state requirement.

Fingerprint and Background Check:

- No state requirement.

Bond/Insurance:

- A $7,500 four-year bond is required.
- No insurance requirement.

Equipment:

- A black-inked stamp or embosser. Must contain the following:
  - ☐ Your name as it appears on your commission
  - ☐ The words "Notary Public."
  - ☐ The words "State of Kansas."
  - ☐ Your commission expiration date isn't required but highly recommended.
  - ☐ May also have a picture of the Kansas Capitol building.

Length of Commission:

- Varies

Overseen By:

- Notary Commission Kentucky State Treasurer

State Qualifications:

1. Must be 18 years-old.
2. A resident of or working in the county you are applying in.
3. Able to read, write, and understand English.
4. Be of good moral character.
5. No felony convictions unless civil rights have been restored.

Cost:

- $10 filing fee
- $30 application fee

Time Frame:

- Varies

Training:

- No state requirements.

Exam:

- No state requirements.

Fingerprint and Background Check:

- No state requirements.

Bond/Insurance:

- A $1,000 four-year surety bond is required.
- No insurance requirement.

Equipment:

- No required equipment, but a Notary seal is highly recommended. If you do choose to get one, it must be an inked stamp or embosser and must contain the following:
  - ☐ Your name
  - ☐ The words "Notary Public - State at Large" or "Notary Public - Special Commission."
  - ☐ The word "Kentucky."

Length of Commission:

- Varies

LOUISIANA

Overseen By:

- Secretary of State

State Qualifications:

1. Must be 18 years-old.
2. A resident of Louisiana.
3. US citizen or legal resident of the US.
4. A registered voter in the parish where you apply.
5. Able to read, write, and understand English.
6. High school education or equivalent.
7. No felony convictions unless pardoned.

Cost:

- Varies depending on the type of appointment you are applying for.

Time Frame:

- Varies, about a week for each stage of the process.

Training:

- No state requirement.

Exam:

- An exam is required in the state of Louisiana unless you are an attorney.

Fingerprint and Background Check:

- No state requirement.

Bond/Insurance:

- A $10,000 five-year surety bond is required.
- Insurance is required, with proof submitted to Secretary of State every five years.

Equipment:

- No specific requirements.

Length of Commission:

- Lifetime

Overseen By:

- Secretary of State

State Qualifications:

1. Must be 18 years-old.
2. A resident of Maine, or neighboring state and employed in Maine.
3. Proficiency in English.
4. No revocation of a Notary commission or suspension or conviction of misconduct within five years of application.
5. No conviction of a crime punishable by imprisonment of a year or more.
6. Conviction of a lesser offense incompatible with the duties of a Notary, during the 10 years prior to application.

Cost:

- $50 filing fee

Time Frame:

- Varies

Training:

- No state requirement.

Exam:

- A written, open-book exam is required.

Fingerprint and Background Check:

- No state requirement.

Bond/Insurance:

- No bond or insurance requirements.

Equipment:

- No specific requirements, although Notaries must keep a record of all marriages performed.

Length of Commission:

- Seven years for Maine residents, four years for New Hampshire residents.

MARYLAND

Overseen By:

- Secretary of State

State Qualifications:

1. Must be 18 years-old.
2. Be of good character, integrity, and abilities.
3. Live or work in Maryland.
4. Three character references who aren't family or employers, and must be Maryland residents.

Cost:

- $20 application fee
- Up to $12 filing fee

Time Frame:

- 4 to 6 weeks

Training:

- No state requirement.

Exam:

- No state requirement.

Fingerprint and Background Check:

- No state requirement.

Bond/Insurance:

- No bond or insurance requirements.

Equipment:

- A rubber stamp ink seal or embosser.
- A notary journal is required.

Length of Commission:

- 4 years

MASSACHUSETTS

Overseen By:

- Secretary of the Commonwealth

State Qualifications:

1. Must be 18 years-old.
2. Reside in or regularly conduct business in Massachusetts.
3. Able to read and write English.

Cost:

- $60 commission fee

Time Frame:

- Up to 18 days

Training:

- No state requirement.

Exam:

- No state requirement.

Fingerprint and Background Check:

- No state requirement.

Bond/Insurance:

- No bond or insurance requirement.

Equipment:

- A black-inked stamp or embosser that must contain the following:

- [ ] Your name as it appears on your commission
- [ ] The words "Notary Public."
- [ ] The words "Commonwealth of Massachusetts" or "Massachusetts."
- [ ] The phrase "My commission expires on (date)" or "My commission expires (date)"
- [ ] The Great Seal of Commonwealth of Massachusetts

- A notary journal is required.

Length of Commission:

- Varies

Overseen By:

- Michigan Department of State

State Qualifications:

1. Must be 18 years-old.
2. A resident of Michigan or maintain a business in Michigan.
3. A US citizen, or possess proof of legal residence.
4. A resident of the county you are requesting an appointment.
5. Able to read and write English.
6. No felony convictions in the last 10 years.
7. No conviction of two or more misdemeanor offenses involving a violation of the Michigan Notary Public Act in a 12-month period while commissioned.

Cost:

- $10 processing fee
- $10 filing fee

Time Frame:

- Several weeks

Training:

- No state requirements.

Exam:

- No state requirements.

Fingerprint and Background Check:

- No state requirements.

Bond/Insurance:

- A $10,000 surety bond is required.
- No insurance requirement.

Equipment:

- A seal is not required but recommended. It must be clear, legible, able to be reproduced, and include the following:
  - ☐ Your name as it appears on your commission certificate.
  - ☐ The statement: "Notary Public, State of Michigan, County of (blank)"
  - ☐ The statement: "My commission expires (blank)"

Length of Commission:

- 6 years

MINNESOTA

Overseen By:

- Secretary of State

State Qualifications:

1. Must be 18 years-old.
2. A resident of Minnesota or Iowa, North Dakota, South Dakota, or Wisconsin.

Cost:

- $120 filing fee
- $20 application fee

Time Frame:

- Varies

Training:

- No state requirement.

Exam:

- No state requirement.

Fingerprint and Background Check:

- No state requirement.

Bond/Insurance:

- No bond or insurance requirements.

Equipment:

- An inked notary stamp that must include the following:

☐ The name listed on your commission

☐ The words "Notary Public."

☐ The statement: "My commission expires (blank)"

☐ The state seal

Length of Commission:

- 5 years

MISSISSIPPI

Overseen By:

- Secretary of State

State Qualifications:

1. Must be 18 years-old.
2. Must reside in the state.
3. Be a US citizen or legal resident of the US.
4. A resident of the county in which you apply for the last 30 days.
5. Able to read, write, and understand English.
6. Cannot currently be incarcerated, on probation, on parole, or have a lifetime felony conviction.

Cost:

- $25 filing fee

Time Frame:

- 2 to 10 weeks

Training:

- No state requirement.

Exam:

- No state requirement.

Fingerprint and Background Check:

- No state requirement.

Bond/Insurance:

- A $5,000 four-year surety bond is required.
- No insurance requirement.

Equipment:

- A stamp or embosser with black or blue ink and must contain the following:
  - ☐ Your name
  - ☐ The words "State of Mississippi."
  - ☐ The county where you reside on the margin
  - ☐ The words "Notary Public."
  - ☐ Your identification number of commission
  - ☐ The statement: "Commission expires (date)" across the center of the seal
- A notary journal is required.

Length of Commission:

- Varies

Overseen By:

- Secretary of State

State Qualifications:

1. Must be 18 years-old.
2. Permanent resident alien or a registered voter in the county of your application.
3. A resident of the county of application.
4. US residents from another state are allowed as long as they work in Missouri and only use their Notary seal in the course of employment.
5. Able to read and write English.
6. No revocation of commission in the last 10 years.
7. No conviction of a felony.

Cost:

- $25 filing fee

Time Frame:

- 4 to 6 weeks

Training:

- Must read the Missouri Notary Public Handbook, then take a computer-based Notary training course as prescribed by the Secretary of State.

Exam:

- No state requirement.

Fingerprint and Background Check:

- No state requirement.

Bond/Insurance:

- A $10,000 surety bond is required.
- No insurance requirement.

Equipment:

- A rubber stamp ink seal. An embosser is optional.

Length of Commission:

- 4 years

MONTANA

Overseen By:

- Secretary of State

State Qualifications:

1. Must be 18 years-old.
2. A US citizen or permanent legal resident.
3. A resident of Montana or have a place of employment or practice.
4. Able to read and write English.
5. No disqualification to receive a commission.

Cost:

- $25 filing fee

Time Frame:

- 10 to 14 days

Training:

- Must complete a state-certified training course.

Exam:

- No state requirement.

Fingerprint and Background Check:

- No state requirement.

Bond/Insurance:

- A $10,000 surety bond is required.
- No insurance requirement.

Equipment:

- An ink stamp.
- Must maintain an official journal.

Length of Commission:

- 4 years

NEBRASKA

Overseen By:

- Secretary of State

State Qualifications:

1. Must be 19 years-old.
2. A resident of Nebraska or a neighboring state with proof of a Nebraska workplace.
3. Be able to read and write English.
4. No felony conviction or a crime involving fraud or dishonesty within five years of application.

Cost:

- $30 application fee

Time Frame:

- 10 to 14 days

Training:

- No state requirement.

Exam:

- Must take a written exam on the obligations and duties of a Notary.

Fingerprint and Background Check:

- No state requirement.

Bond/Insurance:

- A $15,000 surety bond is required.

- No insurance requirement.

Equipment:

- An ink stamp.

Length of Commission:

- 4 years

NEVADA

Overseen By:

- Secretary of State

State Qualifications:

1. Must be 18 years-old.
2. A resident of Nevada, or living in a neighboring state and working in Nevada.
3. A US citizen or a lawfully-admitted permanent resident alien.
4. Possess civil rights.
5. Cannot hold a public office.

Cost:

- $35 application fee
- $45 exam fee

Time Frame:

- 3 to 4 weeks

Training:

- A state-approved three-hour course is required.

Exam:

- Must pass an online exam.

Fingerprint and Background Check:

- Fingerprints are required.

- No state requirements for a background check.

Bond/Insurance:

- A $10,000 surety bond is required.
- No insurance requirement.

Equipment:

- A rubber ink stamp.
- A journal of all Notarial assignments.

Length of Commission:

- 4 years

Overseen By:

- Department of State

State Qualifications:

1. Must be 18 years-old.
2. A resident of New Hampshire endorsed by two New Hampshire Notaries in good standing and registered to vote in the state.
3. No previous criminal convictions.

Cost:

- $75 application fee

Time Frame:

- 8 to 10 weeks

Training:

- No state requirement.

Exam:

- No state requirement.

Fingerprint and Background Check:

- Must complete a State Police Records Check Form

Bond/Insurance:

- No bond or insurance requirements.

Equipment:

- Either a rubber stamp inked seal or an embosser.

Length of Commission:

- 5 years

NEW JERSEY

Overseen By:

- Department of State

State Qualifications:

1. Must be 18 years-old.
2. A resident of New Jersey or a neighboring state and employed in New Jersey.
3. No conviction of a crime.

Cost:

- $25 application fee

Time Frame:

- Varies

Training:

- No state requirements.

Exam:

- No state requirements.

Fingerprint and Background Check:

- No state requirements.

Bond/Insurance:

- No bond or insurance requirements.

Equipment:

- A rubber stamp ink seal is recommended, but not required.

Length of Commission:

- 5 years

NEW MEXICO

Overseen By:

- Secretary of State

State Qualifications:

1. A resident of New Mexico.
2. Must be 18 years-old.
3. Able to read and write English.
4. Never convicted of or plead guilty or no contest to a felony.
5. No revocation of Notary commission within five years of applying.

Cost:

- $20 application fee

Time Frame:

- 2 to 10 weeks

Training:

- No state requirement.

Exam:

- No state requirement.

Fingerprint and Background Check:

- No state requirement.

Bond/Insurance:

- A $10,000 surety bond is required.

- No insurance requirement.

Equipment:

- A rubber stamp or embosser must include the following:
    - ☐ Applicant's name
    - ☐ The words: "Notary Public - State of New Mexico."
    - ☐ The words: "My commission expires (date)"

Length of Commission:

- 4 years

Overseen By:

- Secretary of State

State Qualifications:

1. Must be 18 years-old.
2. Be of good moral character.
3. Reside within the state or maintain a business in the state.
4. Have a "common school education."
5. A US citizen or legal permanent resident.
6. No felony conviction or misdemeanor conviction unless an executive pardon or a parole board certificate of good conduct.

Cost:

- $60 application cost
- $15 exam fee

Time Frame:

- 4 to 6 weeks

Training:

- No state requirements.

Exam:

- Must pass a one-hour, closed book, proctored exam. Those who passed the civil service promotional exam are exempt.

Fingerprint and Background Check:

- No state requirements.

Bond/Insurance:

- No bond or insurance requirements.

Equipment:

- No set requirements.

Length of Commission:

- 4 years

Overseen By:

- Secretary of State

State Qualifications:

1. Must be 18 years-old.
2. Must reside in the state or regularly conduct business in the state.
3. Must legally reside in the US.
4. Able to read, write, and speak English.
5. A high school diploma or equivalent.
6. 10 years since incarceration, probation, or parole.

Cost:

- $50 application fee

Time Frame:

- Up to 2 weeks

Training:

- A six-hour training course at a local community college is required. Attorneys are exempt.

Exam:

- Must pass a state exam.

Fingerprint and Background Check:

- No state requirement.

Bond/Insurance:

- No bond or insurance requirements.

Equipment:

- A stamp or embosser seal. Must contain the following:
  - ☐ Your name as it appears on the commission
  - ☐ The words "Notary Public."
  - ☐ The name of the county where you were commissioned using the word "County" or "Co."
  - ☐ The word "North Carolina" or "NC."

Length of Commission:

- 4 years

Overseen By:

- Secretary of State

State Qualifications:

1. Must be 18 years-old.
2. A US citizen or permanent legal resident.
3. A resident of North Dakota, having a place of business in the state or residing in a county of a state that borders North Dakota and reciprocates Notary commissions.
4. Able to read and write English.
5. No disqualification to receive a commission on legal grounds.

Cost:

- $36 application fee

Time Frame:

- Varies

Training:

- No state requirements.

Exam:

- No state requirements.

Fingerprint and Background Check:

- No state requirements.

Bond/Insurance:

- A $7,500 surety bond is required.
- No insurance requirements.

Equipment:

- A photographically-reproducible stamping device.

Length of Commission:

- 6 years

Overseen By:

- Secretary of State

State Qualifications:

1. Must be 18 years-old.
2. A resident of Ohio or a non-resident attorney who practices in Ohio, and whose business and/or practice is in Ohio.

Cost:

- Varies by county

Time Frame:

- Timing can vary based on county.

Training:

- Some counties require training.

Exam:

- Some counties require an exam.

Fingerprint and Background Check:

- No state requirement.

Bond/Insurance:

- No bond or insurance requirements.

Equipment:

- Rubber stamp or embosser seal. Must include the following:

- [ ] The Notary's name
- [ ] The words "Notary Public" or "Notarial Seal."
- [ ] The words "State of Ohio."
- A journal of Notarial acts is required.

Length of Commission:

- 5 years, unless you are an attorney

Oklahoma

Overseen By:

- Secretary of State

State Qualifications:

1. A US citizen.
2. A legal resident of Oklahoma or someone employed in Oklahoma.
3. Must be 18 years-old.

Cost:

- $25 application fee
- $10 filing fee

Time Frame:

- 2 to 10 weeks

Training:

- No state requirement.

Exam:

- No state requirement.

Fingerprint and Background Check:

- No state requirement.

Bond/Insurance:

- A $1,000 surety bond is required.
- No insurance requirement.

Equipment:

- Rubber stamp or embosser seal and must include the following:
  - ☐ The Notary's name
  - ☐ The words "Notary Public."
  - ☐ The words "State of Oklahoma."

Length of Commission:

- 4 years

OREGON

Overseen By:

- Secretary of State

State Qualifications:

1. Must be 18 years-old.
2. Able to read and write English.
3. Live or work in Oregon.
4. No felony conviction or committed a crime of fraud, dishonesty, or deceit in 10 years prior to application.
5. No revocation of Notary commission within 10 years of application.

Cost:

- $40 application fee

Time Frame:

- Varies

Training:

- A mandatory state training needs to be completed within six months before applying.

Exam:

- Must pass a state exam.

Fingerprint and Background Check:

- No state requirements.

Bond/Insurance:

- No bond or insurance requirements.

Equipment:

- A rubber stamp ink seal.

- A journal of Notarial acts is required.

Length of Commission:

- 4 years

Overseen By:

- Department of State

State Qualifications:

1. Must be 18 years-old.
2. A US citizen or legal permanent resident.
3. A resident of the commonwealth or employed at a physical address.
4. Able to read and write in English.

Cost:

- $42 application fee
- $65 exam fee

Time Frame:

- 4 to 6 weeks

Training:

- A pre-approved three-hour training course within six months prior to submitting your application.

Exam:

- Must pass a state exam.

Fingerprint and Background Check:

- No state requirement.

Bond/Insurance:

- A $10,000 4-year surety bond is required.
- No insurance requirement.

Equipment:

- A Notary seal stamp
- A journal
- Certificates

Length of Commission:

- 4 years

RHODE ISLAND

Overseen By:

- Secretary of State

State Qualifications:

1. A registered voter in Rhode Island, or a member of the Rhode Island Bar.

Cost:

- $80 application fee

Time Frame:

- About 3 weeks

Training:

- No state requirements.

Exam:

- No state requirements.

Fingerprint and Background Check:

- No state requirements.

Bond/Insurance:

- No bond or insurance requirements.

Equipment:

- A rubber stamp ink seal or an embosser.

Length of Commission:

- 4 years

SOUTH CAROLINA

Overseen By:

- Secretary of State

State Qualifications:

1. Must be 18 years-old.
2. A resident of South Carolina.
3. A registered voter in South Carolina.
4. Able to read and write English.
5. Can't be under a court order for mental incompetence.
6. Cannot be serving a term of imprisonment for a crime.
7. No felony conviction or offense against election laws, unless served a full sentence or received a pardon.

Cost:

- $25 application fee

Time Frame:

- 2 to 6 weeks

Training:

- No state requirement.

Exam:

- No state requirement.

Fingerprint and Background Check:

- No state requirement.

Bond/Insurance:

- No bond or insurance requirements.

Equipment:

- An official seal of office in the form of an ink stamp or embosser.

Length of Commission:

- 10 years

Overseen By:

- Secretary of State

State Qualifications:

1. A permanent resident of South Dakota, or a bordering county that has a place of business within the state.
2. No felony conviction.

Cost:

- $30 application fee

Time Frame:

- Varies

Training:

- No state requirement.

Exam:

- No state requirement.

Fingerprint and Background Check:

- No state requirement.

Bond/Insurance:

- A $5,000 surety bond is required.
- No insurance requirements.

Equipment:

- Three types of seal choices:

☐ A rubber stamp ink seal

☐ An embosser

☐ Self-inking "perma-stamp" seal

Length of Commission:

- 6 years

TENNESSEE

Overseen By:

- Secretary of State

State Qualifications:

1. Must be 18 years-old.
2. Reside in Tennessee or maintain a principal place of business.
3. A US citizen or legal permanent resident.
4. Able to read and write English.

Cost:

- $12 application fee

Time Frame:

- Varies based on county.

Training:

- No state requirement.

Exam:

- No state requirement.

Fingerprint and Background Check:

- No state requirement.

Bond/Insurance:

- A $10,000 surety bond is required.
- No insurance requirement.

Equipment:

- The Notary seal must be a circular, inked rubber stamp with the following:
  - ☐ Your name at the top
  - ☐ The name of the county in which you were elected as a Notary
  - ☐ The phrase: "State of Tennessee Notary Public" or "Tennessee Notary Public" at the bottom or middle respectively
- It cannot contain the following:
  - ☐ Black or yellow ink
  - ☐ Your commission expiration date
- A Notary journal must be kept.

Length of Commission:

- Varies by county

TEXAS

Overseen By:

- Secretary of State

State Qualifications:

1. Must be 18 years-old.
2. Must reside in the state of Texas.
3. Cannot be convicted of a felony or a crime involving moral turpitude that hasn't been dismissed or discharged by law.

Cost:

- $21 filing fee

Time Frame:

- 30 days to 2 weeks

Training:

- No state requirement.

Exam:

- No state requirement.

Fingerprint and Background Check:

- No state requirement.

Bond/Insurance:

- A $10,000 surety bond is required.
- No insurance requirement.

Equipment:

- A Notary seal
- A journal
- A fee schedule

Length of Commission:

- 4 years

UTAH

Overseen By:

- Notary Office

State Qualifications:

1. Must be 18 years-old.
2. A resident for 30 days before applying.
3. Able to read, write, and understand English.
4. A US citizen or a permanent resident status.
5. No lifetime felony convictions or revocation of a Notary commission.

Cost:

- $95 application fee
- $40 testing fee

Time Frame:

- 1 to 2 weeks

Training:

- No state requirement.

Exam:

- Must pass a state exam.

Fingerprint and Background Check:

- No state requirement.

Bond/Insurance:

- A $5,000 four-year surety bond is required.

- No insurance requirement.

Equipment:

- Notary seal is required and must have the following:
  - ☐ Purple-inked stamp
  - ☐ Your name as it appears on your commission
  - ☐ The words "Notary Public."
  - ☐ The words "State of Utah."
  - ☐ The statement: "My commission expires on (date)"
  - ☐ Your commission number
  - ☐ A facsimile of the Great Seal of Utah

Length of Commission:

- Varies

VERMONT

Overseen By:

- Secretary of State

State Qualifications:

- None stated

Cost:

- $30 filing fee

Time Frame:

- Varies

Training:

- No state requirement.

Exam:

- No state requirement.

Fingerprint and Background Check:

- No state requirement.

Bond/Insurance:

- No bond or insurance requirements.

Equipment:

- No specific requirements.

Length of Commission:

- Varies

VIRGINIA

Overseen By:

- Secretary of the Commonwealth

State Qualifications:

1. Must be 18 years-old.
2. Able to read and write English.
3. A legal resident of the US.
4. Live or work in the Commonwealth of Virginia.
5. No felony conviction unless rights have been restored.

Cost:

- $45 application fee
- $10 oath fee

Time Frame:

- 2 to 3 weeks

Training:

- No state requirement.

Exam:

- No state requirement.

Fingerprint and Background Check:

- No state requirement.

Bond/Insurance:

- No bond or insurance requirements.

Equipment:

- An inked stamp or embosser that must be sharp, legible, permanent, and photographically-reproducible. The seal must include the following:
  - ☐ The Notary's name
  - ☐ The words "Notary Public."
  - ☐ The words "Commonwealth of Virginia."
  - ☐ The statement "My commission expires (date)"
  - ☐ Commission number

Length of Commission:

- 4 years

WASHINGTON

Overseen By:

- Department of Licensing

State Qualifications:

1. Must be 18 years-old.
2. A US citizen or permanent legal resident.
3. Live in the state, or have a place of business there.
4. Able to read and write English.

Cost:

- $30 application fee

Time Frame:

- 2 to 4 weeks

Training:

- No state requirement.

Exam:

- No state requirement.

Fingerprint and Background Check:

- No state requirement.

Bond/Insurance:

- A $10,000 surety bond is required.
- No insurance requirements.

Equipment:

- An official seal
- A Notary journal

Length of Commission:

- 4 years

WEST VIRGINIA

Overseen By:

- Secretary of State

State Qualifications:

1. Must be 18 years-old.
2. A US citizen or permanent resident.
3. A resident, or a place of business in West Virginia.
4. High school diploma or the equivalent.
5. No felony conviction.

Cost:

- $52 application fee

Time Frame:

- 2 weeks

Training:

- No training is required, but you must take an oath.

Exam:

- No state requirement.

Fingerprint and Background Check:

- No state requirement.

Bond/Insurance:

- No bond or insurance requirements.

Equipment:

- A rubber stamp ink seal.

Length of Commission:

- 5 years

WISCONSIN

Overseen By:

- Department of Financial Institutions

State Qualifications:

1. Must be 18 years-old.

2. A resident of the US.

3. The equivalent of an eighth-grade education.

4. No felony conviction or a misdemeanor of violating the public trust, unless a conviction is pardoned.

Cost:

- $20 filing fee

Time Frame:

- Varies, but generally about 2 weeks.

Training:

- Must take a tutorial.

Exam:

- Must pass a final assessment exam with 90% or better.

Fingerprint and Background Check:

- No state requirement.

Bond/Insurance:

- A $500 surety bond is required.

- No insurance requirements.

Equipment:

- A rubber stamp or embosser seal. Must include the following:
  - ☐ The Notary's name
  - ☐ The words "Notary Public."
  - ☐ The words "State of Wisconsin."

Length of Commission:

- 4 years unless you practice law in Wisconsin and apply for a permanent commission.

WYOMING

Overseen By:

- Secretary of State

State Qualifications:

1. Must be 18 years-old.
2. A resident of Wisconsin and the county of application.
3. Able to read and write English.
4. No felony conviction unless civil and political rights are restored.

Cost:

- $30 application fee

Time Frame:

- 3 to 5 days

Training:

- No state requirements.

Exam:

- No state requirements.

Fingerprint and Background Check:

- No state requirements.

Bond/Insurance:

- A $500 surety bond is required.
- No insurance requirements.

Equipment:

- A rubber stamp ink seal or an embosser with photographically-reproducible seal impressions.

Length of Commission:

- 4 years

Made in the USA
Coppell, TX
18 October 2020